Published by Parnilis Media
www.parnilis.com
and Media, Pennsylvania.

ISBN: 0692587500
ISBN-13: 978-0692587508

SECOND

HAND

FATE

POEMS
BY
SIBELAN FORRESTER

CONTENTS

Second-Hand Fates

My friend is wary of second-hand clothes,
says, "Who knows whose bad luck twisted
into this one?—It's just as bad
as picking up money you find lying in the street!"
The higher the denomination, I guess,
the bigger the sin
someone was hoping to expiate.

But I say no:
the purchase cleanses clothing,
anonymous cash that works for anyone.
This skirt is as new as the day
it left the machine of the underpaid
sixteen-year-old who sewed
its final seams—if you want
to fret about whose fate you're pulling on!

Or maybe I'm always dressing in
someone else's destiny, and speaking
with someone else's words—
I go about clad in scare quotes
and have simply become too accustomed
to the planets and cards and tea leaves
and lines on both my palms—or even,
who knows, lines on the soles of my feet
although these shoes were new—
to wonder what might be sinking in
from all the signs and remnants
of someone's life
that I'm recycling.

September 2

September second says: don't worry,
summer will never end.
Smeary, soggy, muggy...
You'll never get the damp out of your hair
once you've washed it, and your purse strap
works like a slimy razor strop. Even your skin,
that widespread and sensitive organ,
boasts a thin layer of humidity.
As you move, you move more slowly
to my attenuated heartbeat.

And this damp, says September second,
is only the uterine undertone
of a fetal perpetuity: the riverlike swoosh
that rises from the interstate
through your open windows, the tiny rhythmic
tweeting of the ceiling fan, the chitter
of cicadas, and the unceasing silvery jingle
of who knows what common insects
scattered everywhere you listen.

Don't worry,
September second repeats, touching my hot forehead
with its wet palm.
This is the eternal soundtrack.

My House Has a Red Door

My house has a red door, too,
lurking behind the camouflage
of a plain white screen: I think
of myself as a pretty ordinary person,
but my front door is a bright red skirt

that swishes when I walk out in the morning.
And I think of myself as reasonable
and disciplined, but the door is a pair
of red stockings as the wind lifts the hem
of my long black skirt.
                              I'm hard-working, I say—
well-intentioned and conscientious—
but the front door of the very house
where I live and where I sleep
every night
                    is a red rose tucked
behind my ear
                    as I lift my tumbling hair
with one hand, with one languidly tilting arm.

Espresso

Dark, bitter and delicious:
a color between chocolate and soot.
Everyone else loves you in moderation,
but I can't afford to indulge—

you make my pulse race,
my body turns fragile and rattles,
you make my thoughts pound all night,
wave upon wave, the walls of my heart
thin to seashell and to eggshell,
the fine lines of the arteries
crack into fractures, welling bruises.
I only tip forward into sleep
enough to dream that I am sleeping.

In the morning I'm a wreck.
I tremble till the sparks wear off my lips
and the stimulant drains, grain by grain
out of my blood, and the crowds desist.

Then I start to imagine again
that you wouldn't do any harm,
that it might even be kind of fun.

The Irregular

Sorry, my dear, it's been too long
since you last brought your custom here—
what is the password?

If you've forgotten it, as I suspect,
you could win your way in with a fresh jest
or a really clever story.

But talk fast, the bouncer is suspicious,
and the waitress is biting her nails,
squinting at me for a sign—

"Is this the guy you told us about?
It can't be that guy. It doesn't look
the least bit like him."

Squirrely

I should get off the wheel:
I can tell it's going nowhere,
but I love the flash and rattle,
the way my claws engage the wires.
Such a sense of speed and progress,
such a rush and such a race!

Of course I have a life
aside from the excitement,
I'll get off, I'll alight
but first I'll run just one more time.

Just one more time,

just one more time

just one more time

just one more time

The Peacock Gloves

These would make any woman a thief:
how they seduce the light, how they cling
    to my wrists!
Through their tender skin, my fingertips
grow sensitive enough to pick any lock,
to caress the shifting tumblers of any safe.
and the blaze above each elbow: priceless!
If I say certain words my eyes will change color,
I will suddenly bloom as a dancer (my name
    will be Lily again),
the south wind will come to live under my skirt,
and the only way you could possibly
    persuade me
will be to offer me all the bright baubles of Truth.

Rotten Ice

I stay near the edge even now,
I never loved the risk
of temporary winter bridges.

I didn't know him, only knew
that he was the favorite son,
the favorite grandchild, smallest
smile in the family photograph.
What was he doing, calling the fishes?

    One of those men's games boys will imitate
    until they know the import of their weight.

But today I wait to see:
after the rain, the ice breaks up
into flutes, into icicles, and falls
in tiny armies into deeper water,
while the wind lifts the cold
from the lake and takes it up the street
into the city. Breathe shadow, all of you
who walk there, praying for spring.

As the ice dies it chatters "Nick Nick Nick!"
in crystal sugar voices, as my aunt
sings out to his lost body to float home.

Their Language

Their language is full of dry branches,
their language is composed of mists,
and only a few old biddies from the islands
can still use it for kitchen talk—
the rest have learned it as adults
and hear it either as the rattle
of grammatical pattern, or else
as bones that speak deep secrets,
so grateful are they to pull a meaning
from the parched malevolent whisper.

Oh I did my best, I came clad
in many layers, with my story
of death by dancing and hearts pledged
at a later wartime ball. I sat
over the dusty textbook, twisting
the ends of my hair, from which
the depths of red have been bred out.

They could tell what I had come for,
they recognized the keys that chattered
behind my patience. So at last,
when the harvest was done I put on
a fire-bright slicker against the rain
and rode my borrowed bicycle
to the furthest cottage, he came out
and looked at me laughing under those
sheep-thick grey brows, and said,
"I suppose you'll have come
for the song," and sang it there
for me as I stood by the threshold
still breathing too hard. He didn't
ask me in.

So I received it at last,
in shades of grey and loveless,
its waves softly pitted
by the frozen rain.

Drought

It hasn't rained a drop since early May.
The memory of moisture is still fresh,
the grass and leaves still show a perfect green—
only the roots are slowly turning amber.
The earth has shrunk into a brittle crust,
And if you press it with a fingertip
or tread it with your heel, it disincarnates
into the finest dust—into mere molecules.
The particles are fine enough to breathe,
they line the lungs, they pass into the blood.

My body's coated by the ancient powder,
I've turned into a statue, cool and pale
and infinitely dry. If we should meet
in some other millennium (burst fragments
of what I once was, buried in a field—
a sudden trove of rock against the plough,
beneath the usual hardened syllables
that yielded to your practiced touch)—you'd take
these relics for an ancient broken goddess
whose features were worn smooth, and whose
ritual meaning would remain unclear.

Lost in Vienna

I was so shaken when the card didn't clear,
when I had just enough of that outer-space
currency (the Euro: half a heifer) to pay
for the ticket the man had already printed.
Guilty before his impatience and the line.
The station itself was rife with atmosphere,
besides the time I'd already been there:
every train station soaks up as much grief
in parting as it echoes joy at arrival,
those pairs, relieved and happy, who freeze
on the escalator into oblivious kisses.

So I had written a whole page in purple,
I put it all away but thought again
and pulled out the better pen with black ink
to add a single sentence. Silly imperfectionist—
and how could I not have slid it into its place?
Did it fall from between the pages, or did I lay it
in my lap, miss it when I stood
in the long skirt to pick up heavy bags
and run for my train with the holiday name
    of Avala?

Oh, lost beyond imagining:
my second Pelikan, already filled with vows
that this time I'd do better! I hope at least
it was a writer who lifted you and set
your bitterness to begin a separate story.
Words for something lovely that is gone,
something I once held but then let slip,
that I so lament and regret.

The Perfume Library

In this house you can smell
like anything you wish: the cupboards
are crowded with the floral labels
and Art Nouveau calligraphy
of vials and bottles, each one turned
so that its variety is clearly legible,
like little metal signs in a herbarium.

Violet and white clover, rose petal,
violet again, cucumber, almond,
damask rose, sandalwood:
wood and stem alongside fruit and flower.

I took a hot bath and arose
rested and fragrant from its scented waves.
I dressed and chose civet: the one
perfume I had brought here with me,
the one wrung from a beast.

My Mother Paints the Flowers

in memory of ACFS

My mother paints the flowers: blue irises
shading delicately here into white, there into purple
and their feathered yellow pollen-plumes;
crocuses, if she gets to them in time, the same palette;
laburnums and lupines, who almost rhyme,
lavender and like in all their fraternal shapes,
and the tiny purplish flowers of mint.
She is an expert in the greens of leaves, well versed
both in proportion and in conveying shadow,
but her true love is blue, the Virgin's garment
and the petal's tiny dream of heaven, its fervent prayer.

My mother paints the flowers, she is infinitely patient,
she steps back often, meditative, to consider
and is not averse to beginning over again: you can't
unpick a flower the way you can backtrack
up a row of knitting to fix some botched stitch!

My mother paints the flowers, she knows exactly
how they should look, and she has the finest supplies,
the supplest brushes of sable and squirrel-hair.
And when she is done for the day you'd never know
that it wasn't Nature Herself: the garden's more perfect
than any picture—until the rain reveals
the tissue beneath the watercolors, or the season
    changes.

Poppies

On Tuesday one first poppy bloomed in our back yard.
This was one of the unsuspected beauties,
   one of the best
surprises of this house, and now we count
   the final season.
On Wednesday there were two (the old one and one new).
This morning there were fifteen (from the upstairs
   window
as I washed my face, brushed my hair), and now
   there are
twenty-three. They're flying open exponentially, hot red
against the dark green leaves below them, behind them,
above them, hundred-year-tall trees of our lovely yard,
the buds still waiting, pale with gentlest fuzz. They open
like chrysalises, the leaves slide out into soft new wings,
then loll in the afternoon air like simplified peonies,
mascara smudged against the redness, the blue crown
of their centers, speaking of seeds we bake into cakes
rich with eggs and sugar. Seeming blackness, seeming
   fur
in what is really dry and dry again: this flower is
   butterless,
its softness is without oil, it is the daring and fearless red
of passion and desert, it is the flaring and shameless
   promise
of California, and quite out of place in such
   mad numbers
in the mossy north of Ohio, and just as we are moving
   away.

Peonies

Two peonies in the heavy glass vase,
stems crossed: one pale pink, one white
with just a couple of drops of blood
(that dark peony magenta).

Where they stand on the table, the summer sun
will never touch them again; each morning
they're gently suffused with reflected light
and look like a painting of peonies

or even more like memories of the past
when two big peonies stood on my table,
stems crossed in a vase of glass,
their petals not yet fallen.

Peonies

Small buds to open: they say
it's the ants who inspire them
seeking the folded sweetness,
each wrapped petal in the package
offering each next one egress.
Little gear-shifts, white- or pink-
or red-knobbed, swathed at first
in camouflage green and wax.
You must open if you hope to grow.

Imagine the miniscule touches, the lift
at one furled corner. Perhaps they merely
happen across, drawn by the scent of nectar,
tickling by the way with idle legs?
Or perhaps each appendage is perfectly
evolved into a delicate instrument,
peeling but never tearing
even the most fragile edge.

Do they really urge the flower to emerge,
release its heavy scent and feathers?
Or are they just watching, patient
till the moment when they might get
a quick sip of the honeyed stuff,
just encouraging out of habit.

Oak-Leaf Hydrangea

The flower cones are emerging
in the shade along the street I stroll
in the morning cool, and for several paces
I think of you, the person who taught me
the title of this handsome plant.

The story of the fly-by-night gardener
who planted six of them in your yard
when the house was new to you. Two in front
settled in beautifully, but the one
in the middle back pined and finally died.

Sometimes our best intentions root solid,
but other times they never find their feet.
You'd never guess a hydrangea
had once stood there by your house and bloomed.

Once someone on the Arboretum staff told me
that even an oak, if it self-seeded
in the wrong place, is a trash tree.

Chocolate as Usual

I'll be eating chocolate as usual
at my favorite table in the corner,
with an eye out for you as people walk by.
The new white blinds will hide me
until you are too near to look away,
and your ankle will waver in the snow
as you catch my eye, too late, too late,
as I take another bite and smile.

An Octopus Poem

I should have met you skin diving
in a pure soda-glass sea: me
in a bikini and mask, swim fins
and broad breast-stroking gestures
to frighten you for a moment
before you vanished into camouflage
of coral and weed and small fry.

But instead I met you in a konoba
at the corner of Gundulićeva,
atop a platter of potatoes (onions, peppers)
and beside two decis of red (I'm so sorry!) wine.
You're beautifully grilled, crispy
little suckers blackened, seasoned
with garlic and ground pepper, the insides
of your tentacles perfectly white and tender.

And when I think that we might
have to trade places in some future life—
the exchange doesn't seem to me
so very unreasonable.

Onion

The onion is growing.
From its original body, wrapped in paperish brown
and just beginning to shrivel,
a series of green sprouts
is heading straight up, in counter-
response to gravity
and seeking the light.

It's not so much trying to make baby onions,
which would be sad enough for something doomed
to lie in a basket, on top of last fall's garlics
until the fates make it an ingredient.

No: I've taken so long to activate its purpose
that it's just desperately trying to be itself
according to allium laws. The sprouting green
is healthy, stiff. I should plant it
back in the earth, let it do what onions do
since long before omelets were invented.

Potato Salad

I know I promised you concrete things,
boiled new red potatoes mixed with the proper dollop
of mustard and mayonnaise, a few chopped
hard-boiled eggs, some finely-minced celery,
a bit of salt, and freshly-ground black pepper
over the top.
        I can serve it to you in the yellow
mixing bowl from Bloomington that I always used
to make pie crusts, though someone broke it (I won't
name any names): you can't tell from there
whether it's real or just imaged, remembered
or even plain made-up, you simply have to have faith
that the potatoes are under the sink, in a white
woven bag (I try to minimize the use of plastic
in the kitchen), have to believe in the brown eggs
in the fridge, the wonderful soy mayonnaise,
the spicy Dijon mustard, the clear pepper-grinder,
the windowsill of little glass herb bottles with their
handwritten labels.
        And once I've said all that,
once I've turned and tossed my head: See, I can write
a poem where you are not at all!—I notice your prints
everywhere: in the margins of the invisible recipe,
in the spidery slow progress of the ink, letter by letter,
in the reflected silhouette in the round yellow cheek
of my memory of the broken mixing bowl.

And that desire to feed you, to show you and tell.

Baking

You have to plan the day before, you can't
just sink into sweet sleep and expect
that everything will be fine: the yeast
must be fresh, and the wheat—I know
the names of the stones that grind it.

You must wake early and willing to shape
each hour to the laws of the bowl and oven:
heat water, mix, pour flour and knead,
cover with a damp cotton cloth to rise.
There's a time for leaving well enough alone

and a time for the interrogative punch, time
for gentle pressure and then for three scores
of the carving knife. And it's this recurring
care sets it to bake in the proper shape,
that releases the sweet aroma, swells to fill

the whole house. I've heard people say
that working in a bakery you lose your taste
for that whiff, your start to doubt your appetite
for the eternal staple.
But I pray:
                    give us this day.

How Burning Works

For that first instant it's almost cold,
what you feel is the shock, the vacuum rush
of all other sensation out of that place
where pain will now erupt and blossom.

The center is gone, a blister, an emptiness,
surrounded by burnt paper, crinkled skin
(red silk gone to brown, purged pigment).
You run for the aloe, you walk around

for days with that tender reminder.
And the rest of this story
is just a long cycle of scars.

Printed with Pomegranates

It's that underground fruit again,
facing me in multiple versions
of its single and classic temptation:
here its firm and precise cheek
glows red against white paper ground
like the ideal possibility of pigment,
all its veins blend in a single transcendent brightness.
Here its cross-section, seeds peering bright
as jewels from their papery wrappings
as if there could never be any doubt
of the worthiness of the enterprise,
picking them out one by one with apt fingers,
thirst they excite but come too slow to slake.

I am an attentive person; I weigh the question
of cost, and it has stopped me in the past.
I have stepped back, changed my path,
doubted the hand that offered it.
Still it seems now that there are places I could go,
if I saw the trees there vividly enough,
and still come back alive.

Looking

Are mirrors kind to you, or accidental glances
that catch in windows as you pass?
Or do you still twitch after all this practice?

What if you looked (who's the fairest?)
and saw no face at all? If you lost
your reflection, if that snow skin and those

apple cheeks and hair of jet became mere
theory and mere story (if that spell lifted!)—
these things happen all the time in tales,

you know. The simple people know all
the laws of physics, and how they impact
reflections in glass, and on demons like you.

I Kiss Your Hand

I write that I kiss your hand,
but that is just an expression,
an ossified form of politeness
(Austro-Hungarian). Of course
there's an ironic pleasure to being
a woman who says such a thing to a man
(especially one with such lovely hands).

If I could kiss your hand
I'd hardly stop there—I'd go on
up from cuff to collar, from your wrist...
Like Gomez Addams, while you
would have to murmur something
in French, to fuel the enterprise.

Ah, if I could kiss your hand—
or even just watch you write from across
a desk or a crowded room, if I could
shake your hand but press it
an instant extra before letting go,
if I could just read your palm
and softly point out all the places
where meaning blooms in your skin.

At Work

I've been at work to make you something old
or rather, new, but with a patina,
something crafted with care enough
that it's worth looking at more than once.

I've been at work on forms and surfaces,
painted metal (pigments veil what's wrought),
in painted wood, though behind it all
I suspect—almost certainly—sun on bark.

Something you can see through,
or maybe something you can't see—
but shapes that strive to echo nature,
granting an age to the ephemeral.

At play with light: the touch of what's visible.
I've been at work to spread the mesh—
not mess! Oh no! Not a stitch has dropped—
I've been striving to work at a kind of frame.

Wet Hair

I like to feel
the weight of water in my hair
as I turn off the shower
or rise from the tub.
I squeeze it out once,
fuss a bit with the towel,
then squeeze it out once more
and enjoy that particular little splash
as the water falls to the bathtub floor
or hits the surface of the draining water.

And I imagine
that if my man hears that splash
he'll think: "What woman
has hair that can hold so much water?
So much hair, long beautiful hair.
How I love her."

Fivelessness
(Funflosigkeit)
(at the Frankfurt Airport)

In my dream I searched the whole B concourse
    for you.
I avoided the escalators and the moving floors,
I half ran
between the ordinary mortals
walking at their slow pace,
I dodged in and out
with the skirts of my long coat flying.
Everyone I asked in my broken German pointed
confidently in a different direction. You know
how the landmarks start to blur? Voices echoed
from the speakers but never called my name. At last
a sympathetic young man told me that international
flights always depart from the A concourse,
so I fled by back paths, passport in hand, past
walls of mirror and glass. I found five after all.

There they said gravely that they were sorry,
my flight had been moved to Omega.

Octagonizing

The year has a Platonic shape
with as many and regular units of length
as we choose to measure and subdivide.
There are the crystalline angles of solstice,
the smooth facets of equinox, the tongue's
tick (tsk!) of old names in the cross
quarters. No matter what you were hoping,
it will take six more weeks. No matter
what I wanted to say, if you wait a bit
it will all be dead leaves under snow.

Why is the ninth month called the seventh,
why is the tenth month named the eighth?
Longing naturally lengthens – we're a mere
clockwork sphere spinning in space,
spilling degrees in slivers. To say nothing
of slowing blood, graying plaits, wrinkles
that bloom beside the eyes, vision that fades.
Just in passing, time grinds possibility
as emery paper can: first it smooths
away blemishes, then it erases features.

Perhaps the same season will return
a year from now, around the same
spiraling curve. Or I ought to be
quicker to catch the red message
of the year's eight-sided sign.

One Time in Paris

One time my lover and I were in Paris
and for the first time I rode the Métro.
The subway in Moscow has the same
French name, "metropoliten," no doubt to suggest
"metropolitesse." The Paris one's quite a bit
shabbier, something like the T in Boston, which
I also once rode with my lover. But what
I recall of that now is standing long before in a pair
of wooden clogs as the train started braking
and staggering almost to the end of the car
as everyone in all the seats braced for the crash
when I'd hit the back wall or simply fall
over—but I didn't, I managed to stop
using the clogs' tips
like those rubber stops on ice skates.
If only I'd known that things were tending
towards this eventual sorrowful ending, this white
space that follows the final punctuation,
I might have done everything differently
instead of holding his hand, enjoying with a bit
of disbelief how willing he was to touch
or kiss me right in public, reading
the maps along the sides of the car,
those station names that still
seemed to echo the old Frankish or Latin.

Natural History

From the impressions
in the rocks that used to surround it
you can tell this entity once had wings,
before its lovely feathers molted...

Though now it's just a skeleton,
the shape remains despite its sorry death
(whimpers I guess don't damage as much as bangs).

A beautiful exhibit in the afternoon sun
beneath grand windows, before the visitors
sign the guest book and head back home.

Interesting to observe the form
of something I had expected to evolve
into the ultimate stage of life!

Yes, I thought it would be the missing link
that would settle me through a happy old age.

You proved evasive and elusive,
unwilling to negotiate and clinging
to control in every part of your routine.

And I guess I was one of those preying
creatures, who tries to devour the head
of its mate, after mating.

Dove

The name of his soul was Dov,
though that did not suffice
to open that soul to anyone.
You would never have guessed
from his labile conversation
that he had ingrown wings:
indeed, he wasn't suffering,
for he found airplanes adequate
whenever he craved flight.

And I might have guessed that flapping
all about him as an example
wouldn't inspire much of anything.
Even if at some point he noted
that I seemed more capable
of passion deeply felt.

And I always daydreamed
of leaping off the highest Flatiron
in a hang-glider, soaring slowly
down and around and down
on afternoon updrafts.
I gazed up at those bright sails.
Some things you should go ahead
and do as a kid, or they leave traces
of longing unsatisfied.

No hard feelings, right? Perhaps
even your eventual fossil
won't reveal the tight curls
of possibility gone to bone
inside your shoulder-blades.

Advent

We've adopted the European habit:
a printed cardboard dreamscape, scored
with tiny doors, each one concealing
its perfect little wafer of milk chocolate.

Every morning the baby gets up,
lets me dress and diaper her, breakfasts
obediently, her thoughts fixed on the reward,
the single sweet I'll let her pry loose.

Fine to anticipate until the Man arrives
in a flurry of gifts and greetings. But what
will she do, what will I do in January
when each new day brings nothing closer?

Every Night I Risk My Soul

At first I breathe with abandon—
then slowly as sleep deepens
my throat closes,
the airstream narrows,
until the muscles heave
but no air moves.
I try and I try
unwitting, until at length
everything wrenches, and breath
comes shuddering back,
one two three, in a gasp,
at first too rapidly.

I don't quite wake, but it must be
that I dreamt a being of the dark
squatting heavy on my chest.
If I weren't so exhausted,
how could I be so brave?
What must the dwindling oxygen
come to smell like, trapped
in its damp prison of flesh?

And how can I relax back into trust
when the night so presses me,
when all the hags in the universe
are hovering midair in line
for their turn
to crouch on my chest?

I die a hundred times in these hours,
then snarl back to life:
no, no, not time,
it's not quite time yet.

On Dentistry

1.

Everything feels huge inside my mouth:
massive and significant. Each tooth
has its place and personality, its fillings
or none yet, its flaws, or its mysterious
dead root.
                    I remember losing teeth
when I was younger, and each turned out
to look disconcertingly small.
                                        I wonder:
will my soul come out the same way?

2.

The dentist, with her slight accent, drills
one side and then the other, pursuing
the telling stain beside the old amalgam fillings.
It doesn't hurt—they've numbed me—
but I can feel the drill against the tooth,
gradually enlarging the space
where new fillings will go.

One side takes longer, and afterwards
she tells me she had to take out
the whole old filling to reach all the decay.
The second side takes much less time,
but I can smell it burning
and wonder what is getting so hot.

3.

Tonight we're starting an art class,
etching and printmaking. On Saturday
the teacher sent me a list of supplies:
etching needles, scraper, burnisher, copper plates.

37

I thought of all those pieces, as my teeth
were drilled and scraped and changed:
slowly evolving works of a kind of art
something like hidden scrimshaw
that only my tongue can appreciate,
since none of it is visible when I smile.

First Poem

Are we close enough by now
that I can write about you?
Not make-believe you, I mean, but the actual man
who's real out there in the world—or so I'm hoping.
Maybe the question is: if I write about you,
carefully aware that you're real out there,
with footsteps and hair and fingernails, can I set
a connection between the word and the person
so my lines can work like a cord of magic?

Because I don't want only to describe your gait,
and the way your dark eyes flash—I want too
to figure you out, to bring you closer,
to write a kind of web around you
and softly and fondly make me near as well.
Perhaps even the wondering is helpful.

So: here is the first poem—sent off
with a flourishing gesture. Go forth,
my words, and do your mysterious work!

Braking

I was driving south on 287
with February in my soul,
temperature hovering
a little below zero, snow,
cars throwing up grit and crud
and several of those wide orange trucks
with signs: SPREADING, KEEP BACK.

You know, if you cry in glasses
you leave tiny splatters inside—
like saline maps of the Milky Way.
The liquid we feel falling must be
a constellation composed of the spurts
from many individual injuries.

Despite the bad roads
I kept driving too fast,
passing each next car
that dirtied my windshield,
giving the wipers another swipe,
try to clear the thickening white.

And made it home all right.
The next day, dry and colder than ice,
gusts blew the overnight inch of powder
off my car, and the sun came out.
The dark paint was completely covered
with crusted white, looked just like
the salt monster had thrown up all over it.

And there it sits as more snow falls.
Can't go to the carwash
till it warms up:
not today, not tomorrow.
And can't call you on the phone
ever again

Living with a Reformed Cannibal

She got me to join the Co-op, he said,
since working two hours a week gets us
a big discount on our groceries:
she loves to bake with the organic flour,
she can make tofu as tasty as anything.
And how tenderly she tears the lettuce
for those little salads! And what delicious
fruit-smooth protein shakes!

I still have my steak once in a while,
lunching out with a friend.
When we got married, we vowed
not to bicker over differences
of religion.

It only comes to mind sometimes,
when she takes me in her mouth,
you know, and says, "Mmmmm!"

Sighting Elvis in Lexington, Virginia

We pulled off I-81 for ice cream and air-
conditioning. As we walked back to the car
Elvis was standing by a blue convertible
outside a church up the street.

How did I know him when we'd never met?
Perhaps the careless posture
as he leaned his famous hip against the door,
young and patient, hair bright black
in the Saturday afternoon heat.

The car said Just Married:
is he going to tell the groom he's nothing
but a hound dog? —I asked my husband.
No, of course not, Love Me Tender!
—said the man who had insisted
on a tiny and circumspect wedding.

I looked back three times to check
after we turned the corner:
Elvis was still on the empty sidewalk,
waiting for the journalists,
the opening chorus of female shrieks,
alone there in the shade.

It's so hard when you're dead
and the party expects you to stand outside.

Song for a Good Man

Writing a song on purpose is like loading
a sack with potatoes. But you like meat
and potatoes, and I know that if I don't
follow the path that offers itself I'll never
come back to that place where I can love you.

Because loving a man on purpose is a lot
like insisting on cod-liver oil. What if
I'm here today precisely because some stubborn
foremother preserved her scion, our precious
genetic material with just such fishy magic?

A song really wants rhyme, and I've acquired
the addresses of several on-line dictionaries.
Darling, I'm willing to work very, very hard
to be a good wife and even to sing something
under your window from time to time.

I can tell this is not the end of everything,
but no new image has presented itself:
as we walked back to the car, all the songs
that tempted my fingers skirted you
as neatly as if we had never met.

And I know how unfair that is: as you
held my hand and started to formulate
a theory about male adolescent rites of passage
I vowed that I'd still write you a song,
because you are a good man, and simple

justice demands that if I am writing songs
then one of them should be for you,
though of course justice doesn't guarantee
a song, or the time to write one, or anything.

Divorce

Here's a poem for you again at last:
an elaborate dance
of notice and response,
accusation and remorse
and all deliberate haste.

The forms all say Consent.
In little sheaves I gather them
to get them signed and stamped,
I pad the path of my retreat with cash.
I am the Plaintiff:
that means, I deliver,
appear and submit on time.
That means, I lament plangently:
Oh, how easy to go back to anger,
the nights I lay unsleeping,
weeping in secret, and oh How
You Hurt Me, till in the end
it was easier to amass
all those regrets and put it to death.

Gradual legal euthanasia
of something we once hoped,
something that made us both.
We meet to put it down,
Since it can't be done in one fell swoop.
I check its missing vital signs
and watch the crucial clumps of time
tick by: ninety days, ninety again,
then thirty: the agony moves faster.

I wish you all the best,
at proper distance. Maybe
we'll sign and then in time
be just friends.
(But I won't hold my breath.)

Mermaids

In this pool, friend, we all have our hair down,
we all look and weigh the same. Each sister a hunter,
each sister the game. You are all my twins,
and you especially, breasts focused sharp
at the dual poles of my heart.

In this game, friend, we all play the same pieces,
we all deal from the same deck, the same chair
where we stretch out and lure one another
with the same goods, no one from outside
could tell our bodies apart.

In this breath, friend, I warn you and console:
I could steal you from her or her from you,
I could steal you from yourself. My mirror,
I don't want your soul. I want the scars
where our hips split—to smart.

Endo Meat

for J'net

I imagine them as bats
hanging head down, growing thick
in dark plum hidden places, wings
rich with my blood. (Bats don't
really drink the juice of fruits:
that is a tale that parents tell
to comfort children.)
Folded in neat as an accordion,
another organ, patient as the cycles
that thump through the calendar.
I'm growing my own lampreys,
fastening onto my innermost tissues,
personal lanterns of thick shade.
I'm pregnant with the process,
all of me grows into a womb,
settles in swelling immobility,
gags on the pomegranate seeds.

Fuzzy Dice

Hell no, I'm not getting in with you!
I see the two squishy cubes
dangling between now and the near future.
It's way too triggering. I've risked

and gambled before, and your tacky toys
make me want to vomit (snake eyes!)
in the grass beside the sidewalk, what
they called back in Ohio the devil strip.

I bet you have Elvis on velvet in your living room.
And I've been there—not Vegas, Atlantic City,
but a third-rate joint just outside Phoenix—
leaning over the green upholstery in a low-

cut black bodysuit, white feathers sprouting
on a barrette in my sprayed hair: and did you know
the word for one of a pair of dice?
It's called a die. A die! Die!

Just Passing Through

The woman leaned into the wall
in faith that she'd slowly get through,
and under her powerful hands
(way too slowly for people to see)
the particles melted to clay,
it puddled just next to her touch,
like pushing into wet cement.
It wasn't like drywall or lath,
but like meteor showers of Braille
that parted about her whole body.

For an hour—for a part of a year—
she pressed in unstinting. Her shape
and posture grew steeper and sore.
The pages of space in the wall
turned one at a time, or by two;
from behind she was only too heels.
How can miracles process so long?

"I'm coming," she said from the wall,
but no one was there to reply
of any who saw her begin.
The labyrinth closed on itself,
the wall had gone complex and thick,
its sediments dried back to rock.
Her prints stopped just under the paint
on the side where she'd hoped to emerge.

There I guess at them, each perfect whorl
like a knot secretly in old wood.

La Lecture Féminine

(Sara Schwartz reads Pushkin)

I hate the way they kiss your ass
and quote your corpus in their work.
The dumb exams we have to pass!
They use you as a scourge and smirk.

You were a sexist little prick,
and sex-obsessed as well. You hid
your soul behind a skin THIS thick.
I'm glad they killed you when they did.

But when I meet you one-on-one
between the covers (mock red leather,
volume nine), you're so much fun!
We would have talked so well together...

Thank the gods that you can't reach—
you're a dead flower, a faded sin.
You're Aleksandr Sergeevich,
not "Sash," the way you could have been.

The Lobby of the Holiday Inn

Across from the pier, in view of the bridge
whose metal is painted a color that strives
to be closer and closer to the sky
despite the monumental base
from which it springs and stretches straight,
taut all the way across to New Jersey,
we popped into a hotel, pretended
to be waiting for someone in the lobby.

My daughter seems fairly impervious,
but I'm full of the lobby of the Holiday Inn,
the fake fire with its artful logs (and real flame
fed by pipes of gas), the non-Christmas music,
thanks be to God, the two big-screen TVs
that seem to be arranged so as to show
the same program with half a second delay,
making every consonant stutter—

oh Muse, I know thou shalt never,
never in millennia visit me here! All I can do
is learn and observe the sort of place
where I could never worship and never obey.

Pulling Trash Vines

Rhododendrons are fussy creatures,
and these climbing vines whose name I forget
(that bloom in summer with a froth of small
white flowers) can quickly strangle them.

The experts assure me that if you simply keep
pulling them up, in time the roots will starve
for oxygen, or send up desperate shoots
in the grass, where the lawnmower
will graze them effortlessly.

I can't always make out the stems
but have to find the paler green
of leaves smaller than rhododendrons'
and follow their tower down to the ground.

But I have been diligent, and the shoots
this time reach only a few feet up.
I yank the roots out and then pull sideways,
and the ramifying stretch of various stems

and tendrils softly releases the gnarled branches
after a moment of tension; the rhododendron
seems to sigh and returns to its previous posture,
and I bend to gather the tossed lines of the vines
already wilting on the dewy grass.

Poison Ivy

1. The First Time

Who says wrists and ankles aren't still eroticized?
They're the first parts you can get to, the parts
most at risk even if you dress in all the clothes
you can think of, long sleeves, socks and shoes,
gardening gloves—hey, I'm not a specialist.

Hauling on the big vines, using your weight
to master them, of course when they snap
you tumble into the little beginning sprouts
that you don't recognize. The next day,
or in three the first touches will appear
like slender irritated necklaces, puss
pearls on a fraying red thread.

Proving who is true god of the garden.

2. The Second Time

Poison ivy is like sexual obsession,
it pulls all my body's attention
to those blistering organs of delight.
My body says, touch me there, touch
my ankle. Rub a little. *Ooooooooh.*

Three minutes later it's calling again
with every seductive swish of my skirt,
begging any passing hands, especially my own.

3. The Fall

I was being so good, not scratching
the fulminating bubbles, in spite
of all the temptation: I was doing
what the doctor said, until

I went downstairs to put on the laundry
and stood for five minutes, head down,
in front of the dryer, scratching every bit
of available skin from the knees down
to the cold cement ground.

Weak woman,
leaky vessel!
Now I am seeping,
all scrawled with the red Letter.

4. So I Am Changed

Now that I am an initiate
I see it everywhere, the glossy
triangular eyes of its young
leer at me from every garden
and roadside in recognition.

All these years I didn't know
what might be out there to get me,
but now wherever I walk I keep
an eye out for that glossy leaf
and tendril, lurking at the edge
of the lawn, the soft touch
and angry proof of my imperfection.

Healing

(a footnote to Poison Ivy)

Once again you've tricked my skin
with your awkward mark, your guilty delight,
and once again I prove to myself
that sometimes the only diet that works is zero.

Who was I to think that I could
compromise? ("I'll scratch just once.")
Nothing will help but introducing
the vile healing chemicals. Nothing
will help but a monastic resolution.

Is this a karmic sentence, warning me
that I am still too given to sensation
and should henceforth and forever shun
that questionable corner of the garden?

After all, the time when my good friend
sat on the floor of someone else's kitchen,
drunk and weeping with unanswered love,
along with my concern, didn't I envy him
because after all he was really feeling something?

It's cracks like this that let the poison in.

Standing Outside the Garden

I want to get in, I want to get in—
to touch the tomatoes and softly release
the fragrant summer that draws me all
into a smile and straightens my spine.

Cucumbers I can take or leave,
but look at these peppers, fiery bright
and glossy as earrings! (Hot or mild,
or either until the first test bite?)

Impressive zucchini. A lot to be said
for doing a simple thing well, for turning
away from the harrowed rows, and trusting
sun and rain to work with time.

I'll pull out some weeds—just that batch
over there, that's choking the radishes.
I'll sidle along this patch of flowers
with a watering can, to pick just a couple.

What are those leaves? And what once grew
in the spots left fallow, and what's the plan
for planting in future?
                    I don't need a key,
I see that the gate sometimes stands open.

Just give me leave to enter the garden
and come back another time, take a part
in its life of so many weaving green strands,
and maybe one day start smuggling seeds.

The Vine

One leg of the vine outside has grown
inside the bedroom window, and I can't
crank it all the way shut
now that it is wet and cold.
I don't want to go out in the wet
darkness, not even to test on my skin
whether the raindrops are all the same size—
put that duty off for another day
when I'm dressed and properly booted.

The rain licks and drips, it speaks
its white song through the inch
of open window. And any planet will chill
if you turn it away from the sun.

The Poet Stops to Contemplate the Lotus

From a distance I see the leaves
dark in their Art Nouveau postures,
pleasantly repetitive like wallpaper,
veined, edges slightly curling to reveal
the color of their paler undersides.
Then birds in flight above, ducks and swallows;
fish that cavort below, or that glare down
at some invisible fishy business.

And each of these offers the person
who happens to pass by a lesson
in how the air or water can hold a body,
in the pain and beauty of time passing:
perhaps this very thought is the jewel
that shines forth naked once the wrappings fall.

From closer up the flowers are visible,
clusters of pointed ivory petals, tipped
with lipstick pink, all bunched or opening
or gradually shedding to reveal a perfect pod
as a bird's landing pad. The end
of the flower's progress is as present as the bud.
The pod is a shaking toy of seeds,
each one containing in microminiature
that same whole painting.
In their long-lacquered genes
they are a window into something,
a shining through the skin of every day.

By the Age of Fifty

Everyone's mouth starts to look sad
by the age of fifty:
even the lines from smiling fall
into sadness when you stop
smiling. I read somewhere long ago:
by the age of fifty
everyone has the face they deserve.
And now I must add:
if in youth we are given that
indefinite, seductive smoothness
and don't yet really look
like anyone, even if our way
of not looking like anyone
clearly came from a grandparent
whose youthful photograph we might observe,
by the age of fifty we've read
and heard of so much sadness,
lived through so much
sadness ourselves, even just
the small kind, that the face
we deserve is a sorrowful one,
whether or not we kept on trying to smile.

All This Belongs to Me

This angle through the glass, tulip tree branch
now highlighted thick with snow,
and when it's warm squirrels run there.
Once one lay spread flat, a skin
nailed there by some hunter, but then
leapt up and scampered off, done sunbathing.
You won't see that closer to the ground!

That path below, indifferently ploughed,
that leads back towards my house,
and the house even though I rent it,
and all the books inside, which really,
really do belong to me though I am slow

to read them and internalize. Even slower
to reread, though I always imagine. That stack
slowly grows as I'm tempted by This
or That author, title, binding, the idea
that I'll enjoy it so and become slightly
different as a person, that little bit richer;

the idea that a kitchen full of unused spices
might lead to wonderful meals, or a pile
of watercolor paper to a bout of painting
once the snow melts and the light improves,
and, you know, all the days and weeks ahead

that promise all kinds of pleasant delights,
since by then I'll have lost weight
and by then I'll have more money.

Hence the debt in the present when I don't catch
up with the happiness I was looking forward to.
All this, all this is mine.

ABOUT THE AUTHOR

Translator, poet, and harmonizing siren Sibelan
Forrester has published numerous translations of
poetry and prose from Croatian, Russian, and Serbian.
In her day job she teaches Russian language and
literature at Swarthmore College in Pennsylvania.

ALSO BY SIBELAN FORRESTER

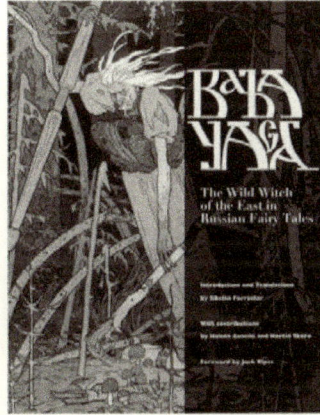

Russian Silver Age Poetry: Texts and Contexts
(translator and co-editor with Martha M.F. Kelly) (Academic Studies Press, 2015)

Baba Yaga: The Wild Witch of the East in Russian Fairy Tales
(with Jack Zipes, Helena Goscilo, and Martin Skoro) (University Press of Mississippi, 2013)

Relocations: Three Contemporary Russian Women Poets
(Zephyr Press, 2013)

The Diving Bell by Elena Ignatova, translated from the Russian
(Zephyr Press, 2006)

www.ingramcontent.com/pod-product-compliance
Lightning Source LLC
Chambersburg PA
CBHW032030040426
42448CB00006B/789